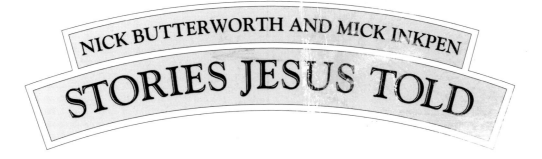

NICK BUTTERWORTH AND MICK INKPEN

STORIES JESUS TOLD

To help people understand what God is like,
Jesus told lots of stories which are as exciting
today as when they were first heard.

The Good Stranger is still a great favourite
and its message is one that children especially
love to hear.

Marshall Pickering
An Imprint of HarperCollins*Publishers*
77-85 Fulham Palace Road,
Hammersmith, London W6 8JB
1 3 5 7 9 10 8 6 4 2

First published in Great Britain
in 1989 by Marshall Pickering

This edition published in 1995

661446

MORAY COUNCIL
Department of Technical
& Leisure Services
J226.8

Text and illustrations © Nick Butterworth and Mick Inkpen 1989

Nick Butterworth and Mick Inkpen assert the moral right to
be identified as the authors and illustrators of this work.

A catalogue record for this book is
available from the British Library

0 551 02879-3

This book is sold subject to the condition that it
shall not, by way of trade or otherwise, be lent, re-sold,
hired out or otherwise circulated without the publisher's
prior consent in any form of binding or cover other
than that in which it is published and without a
similar condition including this condition being
imposed on the subsequent purchaser.

All rights reserved. No part of this publication may be
reproduced, stored in a retrieval system, or transmitted,
in any form or by any means, electronic, mechanical,
photocopying, recording or otherwise, without the prior
permission of the publishers.

Printed and bound in **Hong Kong**

The Good Stranger

Nick Butterworth and Mick Inkpen

HarperCollins*Publishers*

Here is a man. He is going on a long journey.

He packs some sandwiches and a flask of tea. Then he climbs onto his donkey.

'Giddyup!'

Soon he has left the town behind him.

The sun is hot and the long climb up into the hills makes his donkey puff.

The path winds between high rocks. It is a dark place, full of shadows.

'I don't like it here,' says the man. He has a funny feeling that someone is watching him.

Suddenly there is a shout!
Robbers! Three of them!

They steal his donkey and
all his belongings. And they
whack him on the head
with his own stick!

Poor man. He is left lying on the path. His head is bleeding and he cannot move his legs.

He lies here for a long time, then, finally he falls asleep.

After a while, someone comes along the path. He is wearing fine clothes. A bishop.

He stops, then hurries past, pretending not to see. Perhaps he is late for important business.

Perhaps he is afraid.

The man wakes up and starts
to call for help.

Ah! Here comes someone.
A man in a wig. A judge.

'Help! Help!'

But the judge pretends not
to hear and he hurries past.
Just like the bishop.

The sun rises high in the sky. The man is hot. His throat is dry. But here come more footsteps! Who is it?

Oh no! It is a stranger from a foreign country. He has no friends here. Why should he stop to help?

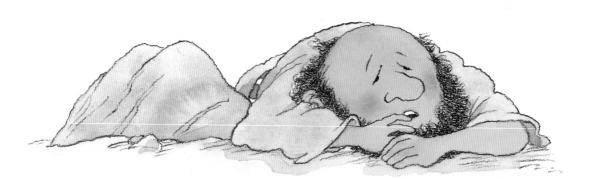

But the stranger does stop.
He speaks kindly to the man in
foreign words, and helps him
to drink some water.

  He washes his wounds and
carefully puts a bandage round
his head.

The stranger helps the man up onto his donkey. He puts his arm around him to stop him falling off, and gently leads him down the path.

At the next town the stranger
finds an inn. He puts the man
to bed and pays the innkeeper.

'Look after him,' he says,
'until I get back.'

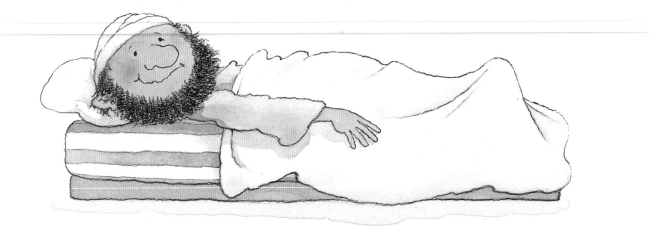

Jesus says, 'Which one was like a good neighbour?
The bishop, the judge or the stranger?'

You can read the story of
The Good Stranger in Luke
chapter 10 verses 25 to 37.